The Leadership Legacy

How to Effectively Lead Today with Tomorrow in Mind

#1 *Best-Selling Author*
Gabriel Wallace

The Leadership Legacy

Copyright © 2018 by Gabriel Wallace. All rights reserved.

No part of this publication may be reproduced, stored in a retrieval system or transmitted in any way by any means, electronic, mechanical, photocopy, recording or otherwise without the prior permission of the author except as provided by USA copyright law.

The opinions expressed by the author are not necessarily those of GP Publishing.

Published in the United States of America

ISBN-13: 978-1975606398

Table of Contents

Introduction 4

CHAPTER 1: You Are the Solution 6

CHAPTER 2: Self – Leadership 26

CHAPTER 3: Cast the Vision 48

CHAPTER 4: Build A Winning Culture 62

CHAPTER 5: The Essence of Leadership 75

CHAPTER 6: Managing and Leading 87

CHAPTER 7: Plan and Act Strategically 100

Conclusion 112

Introduction

One of my favorite movies is Troy. In the beginning of the movie a young kid helping Achilles prepare for battle says "The Thessalonian you're fighting is the biggest man I've ever seen. I wouldn't want to fight him." Achilles replies, "That's why no one will remember your name." He then rides off to demolish the huge Thessalonian. That moment was the beginning of his legacy.

As a leader, you will be remembered for the battles you are willing to fight, how you respond to your people, and your ability to execute. What will your legacy be? Do you focus more on your title or the lives you are able to impact because of it? What will be carved in the hearts of the people that you lead? Is your intention to serve or be served? How do you want to be remembered? Every decision you make should come from a place of leading today with tomorrow in mind. Leadership is a seed that reproduces after itself. The only way to truly leave your mark in this world is to ensure that what you demonstrate as a leader takes root in others. Are you right now the person you need to be, to create a legacy for generations to come? As a leader, what flows out of you flows into others. Investing in your personal development benefits you and everyone you influence. If you want to reach your full potential as a leader you must discover who you are, and what purpose you were created to fulfill.

Once you do, you will become a fearless leader who, like Achilles, will be referenced throughout history. Throughout this book, you will be introduced to concepts and practical applications that focus on developing yourself and others within your organization to effectively groom, guide, grow, and generate leaders.

CHAPTER 1
You Are the Solution

It all starts with you. Right here and right now. There is no better time than the present. The longer you wait, the possibility of you becoming who you were created to be dwindles. You were specifically designed to fix a problem that exists in the world today. You were entrusted with a gift to serve the world. When you find the gift, you discover your leadership. There will be no need to look outside of yourself because everything you need is supplied within you. It's time to stop looking for a blessing and be the blessing. JFK said it best "Ask not what your country can do for you but ask what you can do for your country." The world needs your gift, so, stop wasting time trying to fit in when you were made to fit out.

The first question you must ask yourself is, who am I? This question is about discovery. Leadership cannot be awarded or appointed. It can only be discovered.

This is a techno-centric generation. We use Google and mobile technology a lot. Therefore, I am sure that in the last few months you must have done a Google search of yourself. It is something we all do occasionally, especially if we are trying to build online reputation for ourselves. It is something I would advise if you want to manage your brand as a way of checking performance and perception.

But when I am talking about discovering yourself—discovering who you truly are as a person and as a leader, it's a different ball game altogether. You won't find yourself on Google or any other search engine for that matter.

You see, the journey to self-identity is what we all go on from birth. It is why you will find your little child try to copy the way you dress, look, or even talk. Some of us even chose careers because our parents or a close friend did. The truth is that everyone must go on this journey whether they like it or not—this is for sure. But what is not certain is if they are going to get to the destination. Some of us end up confused along the way. Some find that their real nature is not in tandem with the path in which they have ended up, and this starts to get in the way of their personal life and career, effectively making them part of the problem, not the solution that they are supposed to be.

Today, depression and suicide have become mainstream news for television stations, because they are almost a daily occurrence. According to the Centers for Disease Control and Prevention (CDC), suicide and depression are the leading causes of death after cancer and heart disease. And we all know that being lost in the search for who you truly are as a person is a contributor to depression.

But when you find the real you, the floodgates of happiness and self-sufficiency is opened, as you start to become very receptive to the positive solutions to the myriad of challenges facing you.

So, how do you discover yourself? Let's break down the word discover. Derived from the Latin word discooperire which translates to uncover or reveal. According to dictionary.com, discovery means get knowledge of, learn of, find, or find out; gain insight or knowledge of something previously unseen or unknown. Discovering is the first step in being a leader. Only then will your gifts and talents be revealed to you. Seek and you shall find. But to find yourself, you must learn about yourself first. This is what this chapter will teach you.

First, as a leader of (yourself before) others, you must separate your thoughts from others. The beginning of everything is the thought. Thoughts are what forms perspectives. Perspectives are what defines direction. Therefore, if you want to find who you truly are, you need to start looking at what works for you and not what others think should work for you. Most of us have been told to "go to school, study a profitable course, get a job, rise on the job, and then you are a leader." While, this might have worked for five people you know, it doesn't mean it will work for you. I want you to sit down and think through some beliefs about life that really don't make sense to you, but which you have not been able to query before now. If it helps, write them out. What do you think? Know that the world doesn't react kindly to being different, hence, the reason we come up with negative tags such as "misfit" and "strange." But it is ok. Many of the people who have shaped our world and ultimately our lives have been called strange. Or what else will you call Mahatma Gandhi who undertook a long fast, endured several years of imprisonment, brutalization, and persecution under the British colonization of India and still advocated non-violent revolution? I'm very sure right now that if someone sucker punched you in the face, you will reply with a deadlier punch within microseconds. Therefore, the very first step in finding yourself is to challenge norms and ideas about everything. Ask questions and feel free to think concretely. Do you agree with the current political ideology? Do you think it is the right way to go? Is a career the most important thing at the moment? You have got to find your voice and ask questions. Now, this is not to say all pre-existing norms are wrong or faulty. The point is that you must unlearn some viewpoints and relearn them based on what you know. Relearn them on your own terms. It is only when you do this, that you can come up with thoughts, perspective, and viewpoints that will suit and work for your life.

Secondly, you must start relying on your ability to take your life in the direction you want it to go. Nobody wants to follow a leader who doesn't even have a grip on their own life. What this means is that you must start relying on yourself. Be confident in your decisions and actions. The truth is, your actions will fail you sometimes. No one knows it all. In fact, that small failure might be a big lesson for you. Just fail forward. In the bigger scheme of things, we never fail we just gain experience and insight that we didn't have before. If you are not confident, you will let yourself be defined by the opinion of others. You will be swayed by their insistence and suggestions on what they deem appropriate. You must learn to trust your decisions—even if they fail. No one is perfect. That failure might be pregnant with the solution that you need. Perhaps you have been attacked or victimized in the past for your actions, it is best to address this issue. They won't go away by merely wishing it and may even be affecting your view about things. Look at the people we consider leaders today, like it or not, they have always been attacked for something they did or said, but still, life goes on. Don't let the disagreement with others on your views about things stop you from living and finding the solution to problems. People will always have their opinion of you, but that doesn't mean all their opinions count. There are many leaders in history who have been victimized but still forged ahead in the pursuit of self-discovery and solutions to the huge problems that we are facing.

Therefore, what should count majorly as you are trying to find yourself and your purpose is your own judgment, as you will be relying heavily on it. Even when you make mistakes, you should see it as a stepping stone to growing, learning, and reaching out to the real you.

Thirdly, don't desire to be loved by everyone. You must accept the fact that even if you lay down your life to save the entire world, some people will still think poorly of your action. Therefore, to be a good leader; your existence should not be to fulfill the wish of what the people around want you to be. If you do this, you will never know who you truly are. If you trim yourself to suit everyone, soon there will be nothing left of you.

Again, in trying to discover yourself, use solitude to your advantage. Get away from all the noise, expectations, and pressure. Go for walks alone. Sit on a park bench and look around. Go on a road trip to be by yourself. If you have friends that are also on the same path, this may be helpful. Try to get away from whatever it is that is trying to get in the way of taking your life the way you want it to go. You need the alone time to reflect, release, and rejuvenate. If you are naturally creative, you will find that this moment will be useful for your creativity and help you birth innovative ideas.

On some of my previous jobs, employees would always come to me and ask, "Where can I find this or that." I would always respond the same specific way. For example, "the peanut butter should be in the stock room on the 3rd row next to the crackers." The employee would always come back and say, "I can't find it." To be funny, I would sometimes grab them by the hand and kindly walk them to exactly where the item was. I would always get a disgusted stare down from the employee. Things will not always be where they are supposed to be. Or will they? Maybe you are just rushing, distracted, or too lazy to move things that are in the way of your purpose. Looking is hardly ever the problem but distractions on the other hand can cause you to lose focus on the task at hand. Leadership requires action; therefore, we must seek until we find. What do you dream about? What thoughts do you have that will not go away? What problem do you feel like you were created to fix in this world? What are you passionate about? What type of work would you do for free? What are you naturally good at and feel that you can be one of the best at? The questions are what the FBI calls clues. The answers exist all around you, most importantly, inside you. And this leads me to the next important discussion about discovering your gifts.

In the same way that we cannot see our nose with our two eyes open, often the things that we are best at are often blind to us. The clues are there to guide your path, but you just have to be sensitive to them. For instance, I always tell people when they ask about how they can find their gifts to always keep their minds open to possibilities. When you mention gifts, many people start thinking that what you are talking about is singing, dancing, musical composition, painting, and the likes. But no! Your gifts come in different forms and levels in many areas of life. For example, if you can read and judge emotions quite accurately than many people, that can be considered a gift. If you can make people do your bidding almost all the time, then you might have the gift of persuasion. The idea is to not limit your mind to sport, craft, art, or academics when you are trying to discover your gifts.

To find your gifts, you also want to look at the things that you enjoy doing. Do you like standing and talking in front of people? This can show that you have a gift for managing people. Do people give you complements for your designs? What can you do exceptionally well without the help of others? You might not consider it as a gift, but it could be. Is there something you can do repeatedly without getting tired? Do you love cars so much you lose track of time when you are fixing or reading something about it? This could be a pointer to your gift. What are you passionate about that you almost can't shut up about? This could be a hint at a gift of yours.

At this point, it is good to note that what you enjoy is different from what you are good at when it comes to talent or gift. You might be able to do something exceptionally well without even enjoying it when it's done. Again, you might not even know that you are able to do it exceptionally well. Therefore, to be a good leader, you must think about what you are good at when it comes to finding your gifts. A useful clue in this scenario is that in this area, you are quickly able to identify when someone is doing it wrong and quickly rectify it and quickly too. These behaviors are indicators of the fact that you are good at something and know a lot about it too.

You can also use the benefit of hindsight to your advantage. Look at your life and think about those areas and times when you were successful—those times where you truly succeeded and felt truly fulfilled and satisfied with your success. This can be an indicator of the gift that you have within you. Perhaps, you helped re-organize a complex process into one that is simple and easy to use, and even far more beneficial to everyone. The ability to organize is also a gift as not many people can do it exceptionally well.

Create more time for new experiences. You need to have more room in your life if you want to discover your gifts. You probably won't discover anything, if all you do is spend your entire day in bed or on the couch or at parties. You need to create room for self-discovery as you are more likely to find your gifts by getting involved in activities. But if you don't make out the time to let that happen, you will never discover anything beyond what you know now. Therefore, think again about how and where you spend your time right now. Rethink your priorities and look for things that you can cut out to create room for new experiences.

Often, we think we cannot do something because we are not good enough or have the brains for it. Often, we look at ourselves as "not fit for that." But the truth is that you can't know if you are not fit for that until you start becoming fit for it. You must be ready for the opportunity for life to surprise you. Quality leadership is about taking risks. Try something that is totally different from what you are used to and see how you will perform. For instance, try to speak more in public, create a mentorship class, write a book, pick up a programming language, start a new business, etc. Will it take some work? Yes. Will it be fun? There is only one way to find out, which is to try it. Will you be able to do it? Like I said, there is only one way to find out. Perhaps, you are good at giving good advice. Maybe, people have even told you about how they used your advice and it worked well beyond their imaginations, you can see that as an opportunity for coaching.

To be a good leader, you must know your strengths. You must know the things you can do very well and how you can leverage on these abilities to create solutions to current problems and even that which can happen in the foreseeable future. In doing this, you must turn down the noise from the outside and meditate on your inner most thoughts and belief system to discover who you are and why you exist. Stop watching and start being intentional about becoming who you were created to be. Your life depends on it. Your legacy depends on it. What you do or don't do affects others' lives that you were created to impact. You are the solution and this world needs what you have. As humans, we have the power to create things out of thin air by merely thinking it into existence. I think therefore I am. Control your thoughts and you can control your life. Answer the call that's on your life in your area of gifting.

If you are wondering what that call is, if you are wondering what your purpose is, if you are wondering what that solution is, then, I want to let you know that you are on the right path. The fact that you have even started to question why you are here and what you want to offer the world is a positive step. Like they say, "the two most important days in your life are the day you were born and the day you finally find out what your purpose is in life." The truth is that, if you don't know why exactly you are here, then, it may be a bit difficult to keep going through life. You see, that's the problem. Too many of us just go through when we should be growing through life.

It is a very difficult feeling that I know very well. You may end up working a job you hate, whereas what you want is passion that is burning brightly, a hungry love for living, and a highly positive connection to work.

The truth about finding your purpose and passion in life is that you just cannot think your way into it. Instead, you must take action and do your way into it. This means that you must take active steps towards the things you want and remove those that you don't. If you are finding happiness and purpose, then, be ready to take action in breaking down the barriers of beliefs and explore many different passions.

The more action you take, the more clarity you get on things. So, instead of thinking too much and asking yourself if this one will work or if you should try that or what if you don't make money from that, you should be trying out these new things. This will help you to get out of your own way greatly. Sometimes, you must take different actions and try out different things to find out your passion. When you do, your reward will be clarity which will come through the exploration process. And it is why I will advise that, if anything catches your fancy, perhaps you see some beauty or potentials in it, then, you should take action on it irrespective of what anyone believes or think. If you have found that thing that is worth applying your blood, sweat, sacrifice, and even tears, then you have probably found your purpose; your calling in this journey of life. In the end, this will lead you to something that is fulfilling.

As you are doing this, I want you to know that it doesn't matter what this thing is. It could be anything from skydiving to marketing. There is no right or wrong. One is not better than the other. Also, there is no scale for measuring passion. If you don't feel it, leave it. When you eventually find that thing that makes you stay up all night and get you out of bed in the morning—without any grudge—then hold on to it because it is from this that you will bloom. This may make some people jealous, afraid, or overwhelmed. It is all part of the process. The ones who truly want the best for you will understand. If they don't, then it is alright. You are a leader, people won't always rally around you every time you are taking a decisive step. Live with it.

When we talk about purpose, many think that our purpose is that ONE thing that we are created to do. But this is not true. The idea that there is only one solution from you to the world is one of the things that limits us from achieving greatness. You can have talents in many things. You can be a travel writer, motivational speaker, programmer, artist, and teacher. All these things might bring you joy. When they do, then, they are your passions and a life lived with passions is one that is lived with purpose.

Throw the idea that you have only one purpose in this life into the bin and warm up to the fact that your purpose in life is to do things which bring out the life in you, while also helping others by solving their problems directly or inspiring them. When you live a life filled with passion, you won't have the feeling that your life is empty. Mostly, it is when you don't have passion for anything that you start to yearn desperately for purpose. Therefore, to correct the feeling of emptiness, what you need do is be more passionate. The application of passion to daily action is what leads to a life full of purpose.

The purpose of being a leader is to show others the way. So, be more present in your own journey so you can guide others too. Life has more meaning when you are fully present in it and embrace it.

I am the baby boy of 6 kids from a single parent home in one of the most poverty-stricken areas in the country, "The Mississippi Delta." Up until the age of 27, my life was spent searching for answers of why I was so angry and why I didn't have a father. Why was I allowed to see so many tormenting things and exposed to so much at an early age? Why did my mother come to me at the age of 16 with tears in her eyes saying, "Son, you are the last hope of this family; It is up to you to break the generational cycle that's on this family"? I used to ask, "why me?" Now I ask why not? My life started at the age of 27 because, that's when I discovered my true purpose in life. I experienced those things early in life to prepare me for a future in mentoring young men that come from adverse situations life myself. I was spared to groom, guide, grow, and generate leaders to do the same. I have experiences that very few have that are able speak about or on. I can reach people on deeper levels because it's what I am called to do. My gift continues to make room for me as I train and develop people to reach their full potential. I am the solution and so are you. You just have to believe it.

Key Success Factors

1. **Self-discovery is the foundation of true leadership.**
   You can't successfully lead others without knowing who you are at the core level.

2. **Be aware and confident of who you were created to be and the problem you were designed to fix.**
   Don't worry about a job. Be the job. Your gift will make room for you. Remember this, every problem is a job which demands a solution. You are the solution.

3. **Focus on being solution-oriented.**
   It all starts with you. People will follow their leader. Make it apart of the culture not to address problems until you have at least two practical solutions to bring to the table for discussion.

CHAPTER 2
Self – Leadership

All the actions you will take as a leader in whatever area of human endeavor you find yourself will be based on one assumption. The assumption that you know what you are doing. And this is a very daring assumption. People will rally around you and follow you simply because they trust your words and actions. They will follow you because they have faith in your ability to lead them to the Promise Land. Consequently, this means that before you can lead others, you must be able to lead yourself. You must believe in your own ability to take yourself to where you desire before taking others. You must believe that your actions count, and the lives and work of many people depend on these actions. You must know that action and inaction both have consequences. In other words, before you can lead others you must be able to lead yourself exceptionally well. You must be the example for others to follow.

The desire to be an effective leader starts with you. It is the desire to continually test your limit and keep pushing the boundaries of your knowledge and ability. It is the desire to become more aware of your abilities and build confidence in your actions. Yet, this awareness and confidence can only come through work and deliberate attempts to develop them. Therefore, becoming a better leader of others requires the mastery of one's self.

You may ask how exactly can I become a master of myself?

First and foremost, you must know who you are and your worth.

"If you really put a small value upon yourself, be rest assured that the world will not raise your price." Be confident in who you are and what you stand for. For this to be done, you must first know your value. Nobody wants to follow someone that they are not sure of their values. If you look at famous leaders (living and dead) who were able to cultivate huge followership, you will find that they are people who have strong core values and are constantly living these principles. You only need to look at people like Martin Luther King Jr., Malala Yousafzai, Jesus Christ, Margaret Thatcher, Barack Obama, and many more that this paragraph cannot possibly contain. These leaders were admired not because they looked good or spoke eloquently (which are both important by the way), but because they stood for something.

As a leader, you need to have confidence in your convictions. You need to know your worth and be able to stand up for your beliefs. When you know your worth and convictions, you are better able to take strong positions on issues and less likely to be swayed by the opinions of others. But when you don't even know what your personal values are, it is hard to take stand on issues and convince others to do so. You won't even be able to speak out loud since you don't know what's important to you. You can't have the courage that comes with convictions if you don't have any convictions. If you don't have personal values and core beliefs, you will only be shifting your opinions all the time with what is popular opinion, and you will be seen as inconsistent in judgement and political in decisions. I'm sure you've heard the saying, "leaders stand up for their beliefs". This is the more reason your worth and convictions should be clear to you and clearly communicated to other people. Also, when you act in accordance with your values, people are more likely to trust you and join you because they can confirm your character.

Dan Kaplan, the former president of Hertz Equipment Rental Corporation and founder of Daniel Kaplan Associates said, "I know who I was, who I am, and where I want to be, so, in other words, I know the level of commitment that I am prepared to make, and why I am personally prepared to make that level of commitment."

Warren Bennis, a leading researcher on leadership reported that "To become a leader, then, you must become yourself; become the maker of your own life" in his study of how successful people learned to become leaders. Warren states that the task of figuring out who you are is the most challenging task we will ever have to face and "until you truly know yourself, strengths and weaknesses, know what you want to do and why you want to do it, you cannot succeed in any but the most superficial sense of the word."

What I'm saying is that self-leadership starts with finding yourself, understanding who you are, what you care about and why it is you do what you do. This is a path you must take yourself. Clarify your values and aspirations because nobody can do this for you. This is the very first step in self-leadership.

Secondly, you must take ownership of your future.

The truth about self-leadership is that it is not glamorous. It is difficult. And it must be done by you. No one will shout your praise from the rooftops for leading yourself in the right direction. This is what leads us to this second point, which is about taking ownership of your future. Most of us while growing up had people who cared about our development more than we did until we were able to graduate from school, move into our own apartments, and start generating our own income. For some, even though in adulthood, parental support is still guaranteed. But in the case of leadership, supporting others can be a challenge and nobody will bear the weight for you. Therefore, you must start taking responsibility for your own growth and development.

Yes, you might have people who care about you, support you, and even want to invest in you, but only you can take yourself to the future that you want. Only you can do the work that needs to be done. If you can take responsibility for your future by setting goals and taking decisive actions that move you closer to your self-leadership future, you will be less likely to waste useful time beating yourself up over unmet expectations. You must tell yourself every day how important your actions are. You must not let someone else determine the outcomes of your life. Be intentional about the goals you set. Let your action plans indicate your hunger for that future which you desire. Let them be timely and realistic. You are a leader, and this means that you have got to have strategies that will lead you to the destination. You must define where you want to go, how you want to go about it, where and how you want to learn, who you want to learn from, and how you are going to achieve these things. Planning is the key and the most important investment of time that you will ever make. You may also need guidance and support from people who have been there. Therefore, it is imperative that you know what you want first, create a plan on how to get there, then seek the assistance of wise counsels to help you get there. Laser beam focus on what you want out of life will help you avoid being a jack of all trades and a master of none.

Develop your strengths/gifts so that you can master your craft and make yourself indispensable.

At this point, you must have probably found at least one thing you are good at—which is good by the way. But what you should ask yourself is this: am I a master at this thing? If you and a group of other nine people are assembled to demonstrate competence in this craft, how would you fare? In his book titled *Mastery*, Robert Greene posits that it takes 10,000 hours of practice to be a master of something. Many people think that having money is important to being a good leader, some even think that being highly born or having a famous family name can make them better leaders. The truth is while wealth, high social status, and good family names can take you a considerable distance in life itself, they are not prerequisites for being better at leading. Roberts Greene explains in the book that Leonardo da Vinci was born as the illegitimate child of a poor woman. By the time he was 14, he had taken up apprenticeship in construction, painting, metallurgy, and woodwork. And by his 20th birthday, Da Vinci had achieved qualification as a Master in the Guild of St. Luke. In order to make his work seem magnificent and effortless, DaVinci would often try to avoid talking about how long or stressful his projects are. He was quoted to have said, "If people knew how hard I worked to get my mastery, it wouldn't seem so wonderful at all."

Today, we all talk about Da Vinci as if he was the only inventor, painter, and scientist in his time, whereas there were many people with skills such as his. But DaVinci was different. DaVinci became a leader in those fields in which he played because he obtained mastery in those fields. He worked and toiled to the point that he became indispensable to the people who needed the kind of quality service he was offering at the time.

A quote from Albert Einstein reads, "Only one who devotes himself to a cause with his whole strength and soul can be a true master. For this reason, mastery demands ALL of a person." For this reason, I will advise that you never throwaway the advice of "practice makes perfect." You can't lead anyone if you are not better than them in that area you want to lead them on. **I want you to see that thing which you are good at as a path to becoming a master and every session you get doing it as an opportunity to grow through practice.** Again, whatever your work is, I will advise that you lose yourself in it. You can't achieve mastery at something you hate. The thing is, even if you are doing that which you love, at some point, the rigors of the work might make you get tired at some point. But, because of your love for it, you will continue to work like it is no man's business and you will get better. But if you happen to be doing something you don't like in the first place; your chances of failing will be quite high.

In developing your strengths and skills it pays to have a student or protégé. Growth is continuous, and your passion can constantly be fueled when you see people that you were once like: hungry for glory with burning passion. Teaching others will also serve as a confirmation that you know what you are doing, while also revealing to you lapses that might need to be covered.

On developing skills, I will also advise that you seek continuous improvement. Look at ordinary things from another perspective and you will see that the world is filled with clues that can help point you in the right direction.

Replace old habits with new ones.

I could have said you should stop bad habits, but I find that doing that is a very hard thing. Rather, the best way to deal with bad habits is to replace them completely. Many people when trying to break their habits rely on the power of commitment and willpower alone. Sadly, this is one of the reasons most people fail, and it's why I would advise that in changing old habits, first, you should look at your long-term goals and have a short-term focus. Perhaps you have been told that you tend to react on impulse rather than after deep introspection. So, instead of trying to become more introspective suddenly about issues, you can decide to become more conscious about your reactions slowly, every day. How often do you interact with people? If you work in an environment where interaction with other people is high, you can decide to give your thought a ten-second pause before reacting to any burning issue. Count down from one to ten, by the time you are done counting down, you would have had a little more time to develop a better response or reaction to the issue. If you keep on becoming more conscious and practicing the countdown technique before reacting, you will find that in no time, the impulsive behavior will reduce substantially.

To change bad behavior, you must also be aware of when you are vulnerable. Your willpower is limited and when you are spent physically, emotionally, or cognitively, you will run low on willpower. You must know what triggers your bad habit. What triggers your tendency to speak rudely to people? What makes you lie in bed when you are supposed to be doing valuable work? If you have met someone who has successfully stopped alcohol and drug abuse, you will find that one of the strategies they employed was staying away from family and friends who also take alcohol. No more social nights in bars. No more beers in the fridge for friendly visits. If their alcoholism is caused by depression, their coach may advise that they spend more time with people and things that make them happy so that they don't have to resort to alcohol for temporary happiness. These strategies are based on the removal of triggers. If you tend to snap at people when exhausted, then, put in place systems that will not support you and not make you exhausted to that point where you descend into speaking out of tune to those that need you.

Accountability is important in leadership. You must be accountable to yourself and the people you are serving. It is even more important when you have a habit that you are trying to change. When trying to replace a bad habit. It pays to have an accountability partner. Let this person know the whole truth: why you are changing this habit, what triggers this habit, and how they can help you. When you fail too, talk to them. They can have ideas that will help you stay strong in such situations next time.

Surround yourself with like-minded individuals

There is a popular saying that, "Your network is your Net worth." Whether you like it or not, whether you believe it or not, you are the average of the five people closest to you. We are an indication of the people we rub minds and interact with on a very frequent basis. Their actions and behaviors are what vibrates and subtly influence our everyday choices. Your immediate environment, your immediate circle of friends' shapes who you are and who you will become. If you look at the most successful people in the world today, you will find that many of them have one another on speed dial. Bill Gates has been close to Warren Buffet as a young man. Leonardo DiCaprio is a childhood friend of Tobey Maguire. David Beckham and Gordon Ramsay were friends and played football together, Steve Jobs and Steve Wozniack were friends and started the tech industry giant Apple Inc. together. The elites know the importance of network and it is why many of them buy apartments and school their children in areas where there are high net-worth individuals like them.

When you surround yourself with powerful and successful people with minds such as yours, they can help you work on your weakness. Some of these people would have walked the same path you are walking and help protect you from possible pitfalls on the way. These people don't necessarily have to be popular figures, they could even be people who are on the same journey with you. They don't have to be famous or popular. They just have to be people who have the capacity to change your life for the better through their experience, perspective, encouragement, and guidance. Perhaps you want to start your own company that will create a meaningful product or offer a service that will solve a pressing issue while staying profitable, then you will need to network with people who have done it. You may need to attend industry events like networking events and conferences to meet these people. You may need to reach out through emails and phone calls and request a meeting.

As you are doing all of this, you should also be uprooting and weeding out the people you don't need in your life. Don't keep negative people who won't value your drive to excel around you. Avoid being around people who will not add value to you but only want you to fulfill their needs.

Your network should include people that can innovate, think, listen, advise, encourage, hold you to higher standard, and more importantly reprimand you when you don't do the right thing. As you are looking out for people like this, also make sure that you listen. Your eyes and ears should be on high alert.

Make the most of every moment you get.

Time can be your greatest commodity or your greatest enemy depending on how you use it. It is one thing we have, yet lack. Our lives are measured in bands of 24 hours and what we do within these 24-hour bands are very important to our success in our personal lives and our capacity as leaders. Unfortunately, many people live this 24-hour band as it comes. Many are not deliberate about its use and it's why they don't end up successful. Successful people who care about their development and growth know that every minute of every day is very important. They know that what you do with time and opportunities are what makes the difference.

For example, my time in the car is planned. I start off listening to a few minutes of music to set the tone, from there I listen to an audiobook or something to enrich my thinking. What you put in is what you get out. I know some people who love to rise early at 5 am and tackle the most daunting task of their day. By the time it is 8am where many are just about to shower, they are already on to another important task. If being an early riser works for you, make the most of it. If you have the chance to have a conversation with someone you admire or even idolize, take the chance. Moments are everything. If you find yourself in a conference and some things need clarity, seize the moments and ask your questions. If you find yourself in the waiting room, pick up your phone and do an internet search of the organization. Let no moment go to waste. When you are involved in a project or discussion with others, be present. Maintain awareness. Put away distractions. Look people in the eye and let their emotions reveal more than their words. You will need this a lot as a leader. Give time for reactions and answers too. Nurture your soul and spirit even when you have very demanding schedules. Say a word of thankfulness as you walk down the hallway. Appreciate the beauty of your body as you open the glass door. Every moment should be totally maximized.

Do things that stretch you outside of your comfort zone.

There are three zones of leadership; you might have been familiar with some of them.

1. The Comfort Zone
2. The Learning Zone
3. The Danger Zone

The comfort zone as the name implies is the zone of safety. According to Wikipedia, the comfort zone is "a psychological state in which a person feels familiar, at ease, in control, and experiences low anxiety. A person in this state uses a limited set of behaviors to deliver a steady level of performance, usually without a sense of risk."

A comfort zone is not a zone of progress because it is that place where everything feels fine because you feel in charge. Because you are not experiencing any serious anxiety and relying on a limited set of behaviors, you are not developing any new skills and are not getting better. The comfort zone is a place where nothing challenges you and you never grow.

In 1908, two psychologists Robert M. Yerkes and John D. Dodson conducted an **experiment** with the aim of determining how anxiety affects performance. The results of the experiment showed that poor performance results in situations of little anxiety, whereas increase in anxiety correlates with increased performance. Although too much anxiety can also result in substandard performance. The result of the research showed that, to ensure that performance stays at optimum level, there should also be a state of optimal anxiety. This relationship is explained by the Yerkes-Dodson law.

The law showed that as anxiety increases, performance also increases up to an optimal point. If the anxiety is increased beyond the optimal point, the performance will start to drop. If you are stressed out or too anxious, then you will experience a drop-in performance. The optimal level of anxiety is in a zone that is just outside the comfort zone—the learning zone.

The learning zone is where all the actions happen. It is that area that lies just outside your comfort zone. It is the place where you grow, where the foundation of your success is laid, and where your goals are attained.

If you have ever tried to learn a new skill, then you have stepped outside your comfort zone into the learning zone. Leaving the comfort zone is like lifting deadweights for the first time. You may struggle. You may lose energy and concentration, but with practice, you will be better. You will get used to it. Perhaps, you are trying to develop better skills at data interpretation. At first, things may look all fuzzy. Bar charts and accompanying data may make no sense at first and may even get you anxious, should you need them in your presentation. However, if you spend enough time with them, you begin to gain more clarity and what makes no sense initially starts to reveal their meanings. You start to see patterns and interpretation becomes more natural. Before you know it, you are walking into powerful meetings explaining data like it's nobody's business.

Therefore, unless you are ready to move out of your comfort zone into the learning zone, you may not grow. If you are doing the easy things, you will not go far. You will not develop. You will not grow. If you look at the lives of people like Henry Ford, Elon Musk, Richard

Branson, Nelson Mandela, you will see that the kind of people history rewards are the risk-takers. Life rewards those who dared to make changes. Life rewards leaders who put in the action to make a difference. Life rewards those who take the bold step to make an impact in the world they have found themselves despite making them uncomfortable.

Self-leadership done well is that, which you choose the right balance between safety and risk, putting all of the aforementioned into consideration. You therefore need to know where your learning zone is and maximize it.

Lastly, lead from where you are.

The perfect time to start is now. Leadership develops daily. To become great, you must be a student of great leaders. Study them and what works and make it your own. Leaders are learners. Commit to growth over time because the moment you stop learning you stop leading.

Key Success Factors

1. **Lead yourself exceptionally well.**

    You must be the culture that you want to see. In other words, be the example for others to follow.

2. **Lead from where you are.**

    Start preparing now for the position you want. "It's better to be prepared for an opportunity and not have one than to have an opportunity and not be prepared."

3. **Focus on growth.**

    Growth is not optional for a leader. It must be intentional if they want to continue to have followers. Once you stop growing, you essentially stop leading.

CHAPTER 3
Cast the Vision

Having a vision is very important to achieving all the things you want for your life: whether personal or business. Think about a vision like a giant billboard of what your future is supposed to be. It is a giant picture of what your life should be. A vision is what ensures that your attention is focused on what matters the most. It is that which defines what you should do and who you should become in achieving it. A good vision should be informed by your past, address your future and handle current realities. It should be representative of who you are and the values you stand for. It should be grand and bold enough to inspire you and the people whose support you need to make it happen. A vision is a big picture of how you want things to be. It is the signboard image of that thing which you are working towards.

A good vision; one worth having has four major components:

1. A story about a future that is big, bold, scary, and compelling. It should capture the heart that listens to it. It should force listeners to pay more attention. Those who listen to you talk about it should want to be a part of it. It should be compelling.

    On September 12, 1962, in one of the most famous speeches in the history of the country, President of the United States, John F. Kennedy in trying to convince the American people to support the Apollo Space Program that will put US ahead of its contemporaries in space exploration said,

    "We set sail on this new sea because there is new knowledge to be gained, and new rights to be won, and they must be won and used for the progress of all people. For space science, like nuclear science and all technology, has no conscience of its own. Whether it will become a force for good depends on man, and only if the United States occupies a position of pre-eminence can we help decide whether this new ocean will be a sea of peace or a new terrifying theater of war. I do not say that we should or will go unprotected against the hostile misuse of space any more than we go unprotected against the hostile use of land or sea, but I do say that space can be explored and mastered without feeding the fires of war, without repeating the mistakes that man has made in extending his writ around this globe of ours.

There is no strife, no prejudice, no national conflict in outer space yet. Its hazards are hostile to us all. Its conquest deserves the best of all mankind, and its opportunity for peaceful cooperation may never come again. But why, some say, the Moon? Why choose this as our goal? And they may well ask, why climb the highest mountain? Why, 35 years ago, fly the Atlantic? Why does Rice play Texas?

We choose to go to the Moon! ...We choose to go to the Moon in this decade and do the other things,[7] *not because they are easy, but because they are hard*; because *that goal* will serve to organize and measure the best of our energies and skills, because *that challenge* is one that we are willing to accept, one we are unwilling to postpone, and *one we intend to win* ..."

2. A vivid image. One that is crystal clear to you and all concerned. If other people can see what you have in your head, what would it look like to them? What would it look like? Your vision should be vivid and should be easily visualized by you and the people that will help you accomplish this. It should be a vision that is easy to remember.

Another popular situation where a leader painted a vivid image of the future to be expected, is the Martin Luther King's I *Have a Dream* Speech. King in his address against racial segregation said, "I have a dream that one day on the red hills of Georgia, the sons of former slaves and the sons of former slave owners will be able to sit down together at the table of brotherhood. I have a dream that one day even the state of Mississippi, a state sweltering with the heat of injustice, sweltering with the heat of oppression, will be transformed into an oasis of freedom and justice. I have a dream that my four little children will one day live in a nation where they will not be judged by the color of their skin, but by the content of their character. I have a *dream* today! I have a dream that one day, *down* in Alabama, with its vicious racists, with its governor having his lips dripping with the words of "interposition" and "nullification" -- one day right there in Alabama little black boys and black girls will be able to join hands with little white boys and white girls as sisters and brothers"

3. A stretch but nonetheless achievable. If it is not achievable, then why are you even having it in

your head? While it is good that you have big, bold, and scary vision for your personal life or business, it should still be achievable. If your vision is not achievable, then you will lack the motivation to put in the necessary work to achieve it.
4. Specific. Your vision should be well-defined. It should be focused enough that action plans based on it can be developed.

Whoever you are and wherever you serve, you need vision to be able to do your work excellently well. Perhaps you want to take your business to the IPO stage, or you are fighting for better academic support for kids in your community, or you want people around you to live well. Whatever it is, wherever you are leading, having a vision is important, as well as carrying the right people along because, the mind is where change happens before it materializes.

When casting your vision, I always advise that you start by asking WHY. Everything revolves around this. Your why is the centerpiece. Why do you want to start this non-profit? Why do you want to go into the food business? Why are you getting a second degree? Why are you switching careers? The WHY is the sole reason for your existence? It is what every other decision is based upon. If you can answer WHY you want to do something, then you have successfully spelt out your vision. Perhaps you noticed that there is high unemployment rate amongst the youth in your area. You also noticed that many of them spend a lot of time on their smartphones and digital devices, and you are thinking to yourself, why not create something that helps monetize the time that these unemployed youths spend on their phones? So, you came up with a beautiful *platform through which unemployed youths can make substantial passive income in order to take care of their basic needs.* The italicized can be your vision. Once you know WHY, you have established the vision. What needs to be done is being specific about the solution and what strategies to employ to make it work, and it is what leads us to the WHAT.

WHAT is your plan or strategy? While vision answers the question "WHY am I here?", strategy explains how you are going to accomplish it. It answers WHAT you are going to do to ensure that your vision will be brought to reality. Perhaps you have the vision of having the biggest patronage in the restaurant; a place where people can eat tasty food, bring their friends, and want to continue coming every day for the rest of their lives. This will lead you to the question: WHAT am I doing right now to ensure that I achieve this vision. WHAT is the competition doing that I must do differently?

What do you do that distinguishes you from your competition? Take Chick-fil-A for example. There isn't anything special about their food. Their customer service and consistency that separates them from the competition. It's the people experience. What is yours?

If you are leading an organization and running with a vision, the following questions can help you decide WHAT you need to do to achieve it. These questions are there so you can see where you are right now and where you are going to. These questions will help you determine what you should do to achieve this. Questions such as

- What do customers want today and tomorrow?

- What are the available choices?
- What are the actions that must be taken today and tomorrow?
- What will be the cost?

The answer to these questions can help you know what strategies to take next, so you know what the future looks like. Your WHAT will lead you to a list of all the things that you need to resolve and then brainstorm on the way forward. On brainstorming on the solutions, you will find some to be easy. You may find some to be very hard. Some may even take years to implement and some may happen very fast. But it is alright. Don't expect change to happen overnight. Many times, strategies take years to manifest.

Your WHAT will indicate if your strategy aligns with your vision, if this is the case, then you will be rolling out new products for your customers, providing efficient service delivery, and creating huge returns for people who have invested in your business. Long story cut short, if you are doing the WHAT right, you will be seeing success in your life. But to achieve this, you need people. Not just any people but the right people that fit your vision.

This is why the WHO question is important. You need support in the achievement of your vision. You need people to help you achieve this vision. In fact, a good vision is one that cannot be achieved by lone effort. It will take concerted effort to achieve. Who do you need to or what type of people do you need to bring this vision to life. Choose carefully. Make sure that the people match the vision and values. The following are examples of personalities that you may want to consider in your journey to achieving your vision.

- The Expert: Even if you are the guru on your life's work, you still need to learn. You need to always look for people who are more experienced than you or are following best practices in what you are doing. You will need help, so ensure you reach out.
- The Meat Cleaver: Of course, as a leader, you need to be able to make others see your vision. Therefore, to be sure that you are right on this

path, you need someone to dissect your plans and vision. They will cut through your vision and help you bring out places you need to fix and things you need to work on.

- The actor: You need someone to play the role of audience, investor, customer, etc. You need someone to ask you questions and critique your plans and your vision. It is better to see how badly you are sounding from someone you know on a personal level than in front of your audience. The actor is very important when framing your vision or plan.
- The Reflector: You need someone to tell you without mincing words whether you are putting in enough effort or doing well in your plan. You need an accountability partner; someone to hold up the mirror in your face and help you see your blind spots before they take you off track.
- The Supporter: On dark days, you will need someone to lift your spirit. You will need words of encouragement. You will need someone to motivate you; someone you can count on to help you stay strong to your values and commitment.

- The Safe: These are people with whom you can share your deepest thoughts and they will not judge you or make you feel bad. As the ideas sink in, they are the ones you need to bounce the idea off as they might help you refine it so that it is more actionable and profitable.

Lastly, the HOW. What I mean by HOW, it refers to what system or process will you use.

Make sure that values are displayed across the board 365 days a year and not just on company picnics or events. Create systems that will help you track the progress of your plan. Incorporate milestones that can help see how you are doing in accordance to the achievement of your vision. Create a culture that will draw you closer to your goals. Reward good actions towards the achievement of the vision and redirect actions that will not. Your environment should also be one that will make it easy to take positive actions toward your vision.

In conclusion, as a leader, you must practice what you preach. You must walk the talk. If you expect employees to put in an hour of unpaid work to meet your organization's goal, then you should be prepared to put in two to show that's how serious you are. As a leader, you need to take serious action towards your vision first, it is only after that, followers will take you seriously.

Key Success Factors

1. **Establish a clear vision.**

    Vision is the foundation of leadership. Without vision, there is no direction. No direction equals no destination. People will not follow you if you don't know where you are going.

2. **Start with "Why."**

    Where there is a "Why" there is a way. Take time to develop your "Why" because it will provide you clarity and confidence in your decisions that will impact the company.

3. **Focus on the "Who".**

    As a leader, you must surround yourself with people with similar values and or beliefs. With the right people in the right places you can accomplish anything.

CHAPTER 4
Build A Winning Culture

Many of us already know the kind of workplace culture many tech companies in Silicon Valley have in place. The 2013 movie, *The Internship* starring Vince Vaughn and Owen Wilson gives an idea into what work working at Google looks like: free meals, resting places, colorful environment, large campus with games and many perks that makes it look like a playground for techies. But Google is not the only company that is popular for its company culture. Companies like Zappos, Disney, Apple, and Facebook are all revered for their company culture—one that both employees and customers love and—consequently boosting the success of their organizations.

Merriam Webster's defined culture as the "the integrated pattern of human knowledge, belief and behavior that depends upon the capacity for learning and transmitting knowledge to succeeding generations."

Any group or organization that doesn't take culture seriously is bound to fail. A survey of over 350 organizations across Europe, North America and the Far East carried out by Bain & Company showed that 81% believe that a company that doesn't put in place a culture that promotes high performance is bound to churn out mediocre, yet less than 10% of these companies have succeeded in putting one in place.

Culture is a very important topic of focus in any team seeking high performance and bonding, since it dictates how the team hires, how the employees are treated, and how the employees interact with customers or work on service offerings. Have a faulty foundation of culture and the overall goal is distorted. In any organization, the culture is the everyday reality that people will come to experience. Culture transcends writing down a vision or mission statement. It is what you do when your boots are on the ground. Culture is what guides how team members talk. It is what guides their actions. It is what decides their level of liberty. It is what determines how they will approach customers, products, and even the community.

While it is understandable that not every organization can afford to be a Google or Facebook for whatever reasons, team culture should still be something that should be given top priority.

So, what are the steps involved in creating a culture that is strong, long lasting that will help your team become highly productive?

The beginning of everything is purpose

What matters the most is the purpose for which the organization or team is built. I want to believe that your purpose is to build something that solves a problem, outlives you, and makes significant impact in the lives of everyone whether team members or customers. Now, with small organizations, what will eventually constitute the work culture can easily be discussed in a round table setting. But as the group begins to grow and the number of new employees begin to increase, communication becomes more difficult and reaching a consensus becomes something that is hard to reach. To avoid this kind of situation, it is important that you go back to WHY the organization was established. What is the original purpose of the organization? We have previously discussed this. Your purpose or vision should be something compelling and clear. It should be original and inspirational. It should make people want to work for you and with you.

Find people who can help you achieve this

Many leaders make the mistake of hiring people just because of their hard skills while neglecting a crucial factor like being culturally-fit. That someone graduated top of their class or are the head of marketing in a reputable firm does not always mean they will bring that kind of performance to your team. Therefore, it is advisable that you keep an eye out to see if their purpose aligns with yours. Keep an eye out for passion, hunger, and fire for your goals in these candidates. Don't just recruit the best people available, recruit the people that will be the best fit for your organization or brand. The values should match. Now, there may come a time when the values of these hires might change or the mission of your company, you need to still be watchful of people who are running with the prevailing mission. If you find that they are no longer running with it, put in place a system of feedback to know why and how to get them back on track. If this doesn't work, then swap them out and replace. But avoid making hiring too frequently. What you want to do more of is hire people that will challenge the status quo of your current team, while still running with your vision for the organization.

When hiring, hire people who are going to bring different experiences to the table. Don't always hire people that are 'just like you.' Diversity will help you a lot when charting out a plan for your culture. You should hire based on an assessment of your strengths and weaknesses. You might be an extremely talented at crunching numbers but come up short when it comes to making people collaborate. For this, you want to hire someone who has been very successful working with different people and teams. You want to leverage their experience to achieve your vision. Diverse perspectives are not only important in achieving the vision, but also in creating a culture where everyone feels like a part of something meaningful and bigger than them. If you do an excellent job of getting the right people onboard, then you have done half of the job.

Speak a common language and act on uniform values and standards

When you have found the people that will help you achieve your vision, then make sure that they understand the language you speak concerning core values.

Think about the personalities you desire and your core values. Do you want to create a place where people are free to explore and act on their creative genius as much as they want or a place where you prefer them to work in line with what you know works? Do you want a work hard, play little workplace or a place where people do both in extremes? Do you prefer a situation where people work in groups or where everyone minds their business? The answers to these questions will determine who you hire in going forward. If you place a premium on customer service, then you will be better off hiring someone who has a personality that displays spark and smile.

Let the values be written and displayed where everyone can see it so that no one will come with the excuse that they do not know or understand. Writing them down gives them life. It makes them tangible. From the highest-ranking officer to the doorman, everyone must understand the core values on which the organization is acting. After this, you must draw up a standard against which you want to measure your principles and performance against. It is only after you have amalgamated your language, values, and standard will you start to see a roadmap to a sustainable culture. It is important to note at this point that your culture may undergo changes as your company begins to experience development in certain areas, but your core values should stay the same. You want to create a culture that is sensitive enough to the times and different team members coming to help you work on your vision.

Take time to reflect on who you are, the vibe you want to radiate, and, ultimately, the kind of culture that fits both you and your brand.

Take the first step and lead

How you act influences the culture much more than what you write or say. You need to show and live the culture you are building. Your actions need to show it. The mission statement should not be the pill for everything, your actions should. You have seen how Richard Branson portrays the Virgin Brand. He always shows the brand to be free, bold and brash. If you live your culture, you will be inspiring many other employees and even attract high performance employees who want the kind of culture you are building. You also need to be very transparent. No one will care if you think your organization culture is great but employees don't trust your actions. Being transparent will go a long way in keeping the culture that you have envisioned originally.

Have cultural ambassadors

You will always have people who place a high value on your culture. They will be people who talk, eat, drink, breathe, and live your brand. They are the types that will always help people see what you stand for. You should value these people as they will be your biggest advocates. These are your cheerleaders; your supporters. Once you can identify them, ask them what they like about the culture and what they will like the organization to improve on. This feedback can help you to better fine-tune your culture. As your company grows, the roles of these ambassadors will not diminish. In fact, it will even be bigger, and you can use them to get a competitive advantage. How? You may ask. Because customers don't forget people who are spirited, positive, knowledgeable, and most importantly, make them smile.

Build Integrity and communicate

If you want people to trust you, then you must show them that you are trustworthy. Whatever the case may be that, you want to ensure that everyone in your organization approach issues with a truthful mindset. The inability to comply should not be condoned.

Part of mainlining integrity is being truthful about your strengths, biases and weaknesses. Don't go boasting about all the things you can do and the walls you can bring down. Whether you admit or not, you have a weakness. We all do. You have a weakness as a person and as a leader. Therefore, you must do all you can to communicate your values in clear terms and in a continuous fashion both internally and externally. Everybody on the team needs to understand the culture and why it is very important that you preserve it. Communication about culture must not waiver. If people can trust you, then they will very likely follow the culture you have set.

When Zappos was acquired by Amazon in an $850 million deal in 2009, founder Tony Hsieh wrote about it in an open letter to employees in accordance with one of their core values which is "Build open and honest relationships with communication." Today, the company and its culture are still thriving.

Treat everyone well

None of all these will work if you don't take care of your people. You need to treat your people well or the culture you are trying to build will be useless and people will leave your company.

When you are hiring, consider character as well as skill. An impressive resume is good, but you also want someone whose character fits your goal. Anyone can learn and develop a good skill, but a good character and attitude is very difficult to achieve.

Once you find that person who is a cultural fit for your organization, then you should do everything to make him/her happy. Provide benefits and help them grow to their full potential. **Retain top talent by rewarding top performers. Everyone does not get a trophy atmosphere. Invest heavily in your top 20%. Train and develop them to lead.** Let everyone know that what they do matters. It was John Maxwell who said, "People don't care how much you know until they know how much you care." Engage by staying tuned into the people you serve. Leaders listen to understand not demand.

I strongly advise that you really care and put people first.

Hold everyone accountable

Hold people to high standards of excellence. When you see it, say it good or bad, but always remain positive. When addressing problems your approach is the most important thing. Be firm but gentle. Set a culture that always fails forward and never travel alone on the journey.

Key Success Factors

1. **Cleary define your culture**

   To receive buy-in from your employees you must be able to paint a clear picture of what the expectations are and what winning looks like.

2. **Hire the best fit not the best available**

   You've probably heard the phrase that "all money is not good money". The same truth exists for talent. With regards to culture, success weighs heavily on having the right people in the right places.

3. **Practice what you preach**

   It's very important that the leader lives, breathes, and embodies the company's culture. "Do what I say not what I do" style of leadership is a prehistoric approach and will only lead to constant turnover and turmoil.

CHAPTER 5
The Essence of Leadership

Leadership is a mentality. It is the way you think. It's not about what you do. It's who you are at the core level, on the inside. It was John Maxwell who said, "Leadership is influence. Nothing more, nothing less". But let me broaden the definition of leadership a little bit more. Leadership can be said to be the relationship between a person (who is the leader) and a group of people (the followers or team members) where this person uses their skills and intellectual capacity to successfully guide the group towards a common goal. Take note of the words: skills, intellectual capacity, guide, group, and common goal because these words make a lot of difference in leadership. For instance, a leader can perform excellently well in one group and woefully well in another for many reasons. One of which is if a group does not feel like they are a part of the leader's goal, which can happen if the leader lacks the skill to carry the group along in the achievement of the goal. In every corner of the world, good leadership is something every group yearns for. Good leadership is what every association, union, and citizen of every nation clamors for, because good leadership touches life and changes it positively forever.

I've had the opportunity to speak on leadership on many occasions and I've discussed and interacted with many business leaders, entrepreneurs, middle-class workers, corporate executives, blue collar workers, and people doing minimum wage jobs, one of the things I have found is that people choose to follow leaders that inspire and motivate them. They follow leaders that they feel they connect to. Leadership is separate from management because, it is not confined by structure, hierarchy, or system. It is direct, consistent, and simple to access and enjoy. Nonetheless, good leadership is not something that comes easy.

Based on my experience and research, I have come to see that good leadership is about:

Setting people on the right path

It doesn't matter what your mission and vision statement is, what people want is someone they can look up to for guidance and direction when things are not clear. People want leaders that will encourage them and set them on the right path for success. People want to know where the leader is taking them. If there is anything studying leadership has shown me, it is that people want to be led. People want to be shown the way. People don't just want to see the map hanging on the wall, they want to be shown how to sail. They want to go on the journey with you as the pilot. They want to see that your actions and decisions as a leader is taking them on the right path. Good leadership is about leading people in the right direction towards a positive goal. This direction needs to permeate and reflect in every decision you will be making as the leader for the group. Holding the light for others to follow is a very key feature of good leadership.

Creating a relationship based on trust

Good leadership is emotional. People are attached to people they can trust. Nobody wants to follow a leader who talks tough and act simple. They want you to say something and act it. No one wants to follow a leader whose words and actions they can't trust. As a leader, you want to get the trust of the people you are leading. But trust takes time. It is not something that just happens to people. It is something that is slowly earned. It is something that is built on honesty and integrity. As a leader, people want to trust you to safeguard their interests. They want to go to bed knowing that your protection over them is sure. The Watergate Scandal of President Nixon and the Monica Lewinsky Scandal of President Clinton are prime examples of the results of the violation of followers' trust. In both cases, people were angered more by the lies and attempts at cover-ups than the actual events themselves. In the 1990s, when the story of trading regulations violations rocked Salomon Brothers, many customers left the company. Why? Trust. If I'm going to trust you with my money, then I must be completely sure that you are going to do the right thing with it. If not, then why give you my money? It took the intervention of the founder of Berkshire Hathaway and billionaire businessman to calm down stakeholders and restore trust while getting the company reduced fines. Being truthful and honest is the only solution in leadership. At least you can pick up the pieces and get on with life after that. In many cases, people will forgive you quickly if you tell them the truth than when they uncover the lies themselves or when you try so hard to cover it up.

Creating an air of integrity and living up to it

If you are promising your paradise, be rest assured that they will demand to see that paradise when the time comes. Fail to deliver on your promise and you will lose integrity. You must have some set of core values that will guide you towards achieving your set goals. It is not only having these values, it is living them. If you are telling employees not to sell their shares in your company to boost investor confidence, don't go sneaking behind their backs to sell yours. If you are telling team members to work an extra shift, don't go napping in your corner office just because you are the boss. People want to see you live your values. You can't preach hard work at board meetings and be spending half your time as the leader doing the bare minimums. That will kill your leadership.

The key to achieving balance is letting your actions be in line with your values. If your value is efficiency when it comes to product development, the kind of people you will attract to your team will not be the marketers. No. They will be people who believe in the philosophy of a more efficient product. And when you are working with these people, you should let your actions reflect your belief in this goal. You must not be dwelling on marketing tactics when the goal is to make the product faster, better, cost-effective, etc.

Maintaining consistency of action according to vision and values

Nobody wants a leader who changes their directions like the weather. People love consistency and predictability. They don't want your values to waiver according to opinion polls. They want someone who is firm and dependable. Yes, change is the only constant thing in life, so why want someone who wouldn't change, you may ask. Firm doesn't mean rigid. What I mean is that core values must remain the same while strategies can be changed. Dependability is about values not tactics.

Maintaining strong connection to followers

From my observation and studies, people connect to leaders when they share values. This is the reason followers leave when they find that a leader's values have changed. As a leader, by helping them feel like they are a part of something greater than them, you are giving them a vision for their lives and they will love you for it. For example, a leader of a cancer research team in a pharmaceutical company can say, "By working here, you are not only advancing your career, you are touching millions of lives across the globe and changing lives positively." If you have high-flyers in your team, you can celebrate and elevate them as a way of showing your support and the fact that you value them. You must also be careful not to take credit for the work of others.

GABRIEL WALLACE

Learning constantly

People will look up to you as the messiah in many situations. Don't be surprised if your marketing exec asks for marital advice. It all depends on the kind of connection you have built. But the point is that your team will expect you to know the work and the way. Therefore, you have to learn constantly. You also must make sure that other people know about your learning points so that you all can develop together.

Adapting to changes

Sometimes, things might not go as planned, but you will still need to press on. Therefore, leaders must be flexible and open to these changes as the need arises. Adaptability to these changes, situations, and challenges are very important in the achievement of goals. You must constantly evolve to become a better leader.

Empowering followers

Another important reason for leadership is the empowerment of followers to take risk, rid them of the fear of failure and give them the independence to innovate. If you empower the people in your service, they will work to ensure that your goals are met because they will see the value in their work. Empowering team members also breeds respect and trust for you, hence, it builds powerful relationships where everyone maintains focus on the achievement of goals.

Engaging and carrying followers along

Constant communication about goals, achievements, and progress reports is a key to good leadership. Therefore, you must work on strategies to engage everyone and let them know your intentions.

Serving Others

Leadership is measured by how many people you served and developed into leaders or helped become better versions of themselves. It was Mahatma Gandhi who said that, *"the best way to find yourself is to lose yourself in the service of others."* Apart from the fact that you will be helping others find themselves, serving others will also help you find your way. Leadership is about putting down your needs occasionally for the good of others. It is about sacrificing your money, time, and resources to help other people meet their goals.

All these things I mentioned are quite easy to achieve on a cursory look, but a second look will quickly reveal that it is not a straightforward thing to achieve. Why is this so? For example, you can decide to say this is the direction we are going as a team but implementing it as tasks and as part of the decision-making process is so not a straightforward thing to do. Having values is not so difficult. Making people see, work, make decisions, and create policies in accordance to those values is the magic. Also, you can talk and have fun with team members all you like until serious stuff shows up and there is no more time for watercooler discussions.

Therefore, it makes sense that in your leadership plan for your organization, you should first focus on what you want to achieve and avoid distractions. As a leader, you must also know how to play to the strengths of the individuals in your team. Your aim should be not to waste time developing their weakness. Instead, make that thing which they excel at go from good to great and their weakness from poor to fair. Leadership is about building skills that are complementary in nature. It is not building plenty jack-of-all-trades.

Like I mentioned earlier, attitude is king. Anyone can be trained for skills. Training someone for attitude is a bit harder. So, hire the people that will bring out the best of your leadership efforts. Do all you can to bring out the best in the people working with you. Hire great people, set them on the right path, and allow them to do what they have been hired to do. If you make yourself less important to the running of the organization, you will record considerable progress.

Key Success Factors

1. **Leadership is a mentality.**

   It's less about what you do and more about who you are. It is the way you think and act. This is important because the way you do anything is the way you do everything.

2. **Leadership is measured by how many you serve.**

   Serving others to reach their full potential is essential to building a legacy. Leaders must equip, engage, and empower others to Pay It Forward.

3. **Your ability depends on your availability.**

   You can have all the talent in the world but if your followers can't access you they won't assist you in accomplishing remarkable things that only a team is capable of doing.

CHAPTER 6
Managing and Leading

I have read and even had to listen occasionally to the debate about which is better, leadership or management? But here is the thing: both are important. One is not better than the other. Although, they both are different on many levels, they are needed for the achievement of your organization's vision. In fact, they are complementary. A successful organization must have both good leadership and management strategies in place to perform optimally and meet set targets and specific objectives, because while leadership is that quality which influences people to act towards the common goal, management is that discipline of managing people in the best way possible to achieve success.

Here are a few differences between leadership and management.

- Management involves administration while leadership involves innovation.

- Management involves the maintenance of status quo while leadership involves reinventing the status quo.

- Management depends on systems and structure while leadership depends on people.

- Management seeks control; leadership seeks trust.

- Management seeks goal in the short term; leadership seeks goal in the long term.

- Management seeks to know how and when; leadership seeks to know what and why.

- Management is focused on bottom line; leadership is focused on the horizon.

- Management is dependent on imitation; leadership seeks originality.

- Management thrives on order; leadership calls the order.

- Management wants to do things right; leadership wants to do the things right.

- Managers focus on stability; leaders focus on change and improvement.
- Managers make decisions for others; leaders facilitate them.
- Managers seek control while leaders seek to release others to reach their potential.
- Managers are reactive; leaders are proactive.
- Managers value results; leaders value achievement.
- Mangers focus on managing task and work; leaders focus on leading people.
- Managers produce followers; leaders produce leaders

Although both are different, and in the past, this difference used to be clear. In the industrial era where there was boom of mass production, the manager doesn't really need to pay attention to the people doing the work or how they were producing. All the manager needed to hear and know was that products were produced in the appropriate quantities and of the right quality. Managers followed orders, organized work, coordinated and assigned tasks and ensured that the job was completed. Efficiency was the order of the day.

But today in the information age, where organizations get their value from the knowledge of their people and not how many hours they can work with their physical hand, it has become increasingly hard to differentiate between management and leadership. People now look up to managers to not only tell them what tasks to do, but also show them the vision for the long term. People now look up to managers for vision. So, the era of managers assigning tasks and doing nothing else has passed. Now, every manager in today's workplace must be able to carry people along in the achievement of the organization's vision. Today, managers must not only perform the task of achieving efficiency, they must also be able to nurture talents, develop skills, and inspire results.

For anyone to succeed today in the world of today, they must be able to play the role of managers and leaders very well in the following areas

1. Mission goals

What used to be the traditional view of management is that people are to be run like a machine. Input some set of instructions, the system produces results based on structure and algorithm, everything works well, and the manager goes to bed happy. What the manager needs to do is ensure that the system works every time. Under this kind of view, people are very much like machine parts that can be swapped out and replaced as at when due. Once a person is hired, they must continue to perform in that role or job description for as long as possible according to the goals of the organization and standards set by the manager. The mindset is that the machine and the structure in place (as in the case of today's workplace) is more important than the people running it.

But leadership is different. Leadership places more emphasis on the people than the machines. Leadership believes that the people drive everything. The machine can be changed at whatever time it makes economic sense to change it. The people running the machine are creative and can apply their brains to more than one function. Machines can't.

Leaders give people the flexibility of designing their own jobs long as the overall mission is fulfilled. Leadership doesn't strive to achieve perfection but constant improvement that will lead to the achievement of the overall goals. A leader holds the people working with him by the hand and takes them on the mission. He doesn't restrict them by processes and procedures. He makes them see how their input will be valuable to the organization and themselves. Not how they are going to work to get salaries. Perhaps, the job was to develop a product that will make household chores easier and faster, apart from the fact that they must work to get the pay, they will also be able to see that they are touching lives by coming to work every day.

Every mission has a starting point and termination point. Management hires people for specific roles and make them redundant afterwards, especially when those missions have been completed. Leadership looks at people from the perspective that their skills can find application in various areas. It recruits for the long haul. Leadership takes an already good skill to great and takes a weakness from poor to acceptable.

The truth is that no one like to come to work doing the same thing every day year after year just because it helps the company. People today want to be a part of something bigger than the promise of paycheck which is management's domain. Knowledge is easily within their reach and they look forward to leadership to give them more reasons to stay.

2. Awareness of thyself.

The traditional manager sees their work as a command-and-control position which does not require them to sit down and analyze their own actions since in their minds, they are only following laid down guidelines and enforcing them. But today's manager must think like a leader. Today's manager must look at him/herself in the mirror and check to see if she/he is acting from a place of fear. Fear is what drives managers to always clamp down on employees. Fear is what makes many shout and threaten employee with termination, so they can bolt whenever they see their boss walking around the corner. Today's manager must borrow a leaf from leadership which is leading from a place of trust instead of threats. Instead of saying "If this happens again, you will be fired", it is far more effective to say "You were hired to work with me, so for us to be successful, I think we need to learn how to work together. You will learn a lot from me if you have an open mind and I from you". Yes, I know that there are always cases when people will not change and remain unproductive to the point of corrupting the good ones. In this case, you can swap them out. But at least, you will know in your heart that you have explored all the options of talking to them, carrying them along, and helping them.

3. Taking risk and gaining trust

In the world of management, it is generally accepted that, you don't run a risk of trusting an employee because you have all the authority; you are the alpha and omega, so when somebody messes up, you take punitive measures. But a boss who chooses to lead instead of mange carries a risk of trust and trust is a key part of leadership. Your trust may end up betrayed. Yes, it will be painful, but you would have learnt. If you decide not to trust people to come through like the traditional view of management, then you won't learn much. Leadership is putting your faith in someone without weighing them down with threats if they fail to do so. You have to just trust people to do their best. This is something many managers don't like and should be addressed in today's workplace.

Sometimes, bosses just have to stop hitting the gas pedal and allow the geniuses in their team to save the day. If you are running a team where you allow everyone to come to work with their creative geniuses, you will be opening a floodgate of ideas that may be better than yours. You might be talking about developing a washing machine that is more efficient and uses far less power and someone is already thinking of a way to develop a system that will make the machine automatically determine the material of the cloth to be washed and the ideal washing conditions while also using the internet to review what people are saying about the material to make it able to improve. This is what leadership does and what today's managers should incorporate into their plan.

If people in your team are finding it difficult to trust and coming in between collaboration, let the leader in you try to find out what the problem is and attempt to find a solution. You should not just read out the riot act, instead, come from a place of concern. It is only when this fails that you can let them know that they have an obligation to collaborate.

If you create an environment of trust, then, people will not be afraid to come to you as a manager, they will not be afraid of hierarchy and protocols, but see working with you as an opportunity to learn. Let me tell you this, if you have been managing a team for quite some time (like a year) and you are still the guru on all things, then you have not been a true leader. You are only wasting your experience and insights and effectively stunting the growth of your team.

4. Finding inner voice and speaking out

The old manager is not required to bring their inner voice to work. No. There are countless rules and procedures that ensures tasks are completed. **No need to come and disrupt work with your thoughts.** But many a time, we go to work with things that boggle our mind, things that are although scary, but can light the torch in going forward. In many organizations, workers fear talking to managers about alternative approaches or things about work that bother them. They act from a place of suppression and never grow the muscles to act from a place of credibility. But today, conversations are perpetually being generated about the workplace, it makes little sense to silence team members who shouldn't be silenced in the first place. Today's leaders and managers need to encourage people working with them to speak up and come out of the closet. **Leaders are great at inspiring others, connecting with others, relating to others, solving problems. Leaders are known for having a high emotional intelligence.**

Bosses need to understand that going to work does not mean leaving your personality at home. As someone who is responsible for people, sometimes you must say what you feel or else you may regret the act of hiding your true personality. One day, you will get tired of being in silence and speak out in your inner voice. Know today that you are a genius and a solution provider, will you rather not air your views and let it chart a way forward instead of depriving the people you work with the gift of your thoughts? Speak out and let your voice be heard. You are a leader of your own life and your opinion matters in the grand scheme of things.

Key Success Factors

1. **Lead, manage, or find your place.**

   There are key differences between managing and leading. Although both are important leadership has the most impact on the legacy of a company. You can be a good manager and not be a good leader, but you can't be a good leader without being a good manager.

2. **Manage the Process, Lead the People.**

   To be successful in business you must have people in place to execute the day to day activities that moves the company closer to the vision or goal. Leaders set the direction while managers give it.

3. **You are what you produce.**

   Leadership is about producing other leaders that produce other leaders that create a pipeline of future leaders. Only effective leaders can groom, guide, grow, and generate leaders.

CHAPTER 7
Plan and Act Strategically

In any forward-focused organization, the development of a leadership programs is not only important, it is necessary. After the homing in on the vision and creating vision and mission statements that everyone who enters the organization through the front door can see a mile away, many organizations fail to take a very critical step. The step of the development of a leadership program.

Questions such as: what behaviors do you expect? What behavior do you want to counsel? How, do you want to help employees grow? How do you determine and assess growth? What are parameters do you measure for success? How do you reward high performers? What do you do with struggling employees? How do you motivate everyone? What kind of environment do you want to create? What kind of leadership culture do you want to grow? These are the kind of questions that a thoughtful leadership program should answer.

If you don't know where to start, an effective way to begin is by asking: what exactly should future leaders working in this organization achieve? Perhaps you want them to achieve better interaction with customers such that the probability that everyone who has an encounter with them will walk away smiling is about 99%.

When creating this plan, understand that there is no one set way to plan this, since your goal is different from that of the next organization, your leadership program might be different too. Besides, the condition you are currently in will determine the kind of leaders you want to raise. Perhaps you are in that situation where you want to turnaround things and become more solvent, the kind of leaders you want to raise will be different from if you needed high growth or want to expand. For the former, you may need radical and aggressive leaders while for the latter, you may need leaders who are more collaborative and can operate from a sure footing. The important thing is to note that there is no skill-fits-all when it comes to planning a successful leadership program. The focus of the program will be based on your needs at the time and the future. If you understudy some organizations, you will find that while some develop their programs for future situations based on current projections while some develop their leaders for now and hope that their competence in today's situation will lead to a brighter future for the company. If for instance, your company is facing a recession, your leadership program should focus on motivate employees, boosting their morale, and stimulating their creativity for the present rather than focusing on solving future problems at the present.

Here is a guide on what to consider when developing a leadership program that works.

1. Create role models: You want to use senior leaders in your organization to raise the younger

ones. It is easy to use senior leaders as role models because younger employees already look up to them for direction on many issues. But when doing this, you must be careful to choose leaders who are exemplary in the areas of interest. You will want to choose someone who has vested interest in raising people to succeed him/her, and even grow beyond him/her in the business. You want someone who you will see raising these leaders as an investment and opportunity and not as a threat. The role models should also keep an open mind as it will be an opportunity for them to learn as well, because the moment they stop learning, then they stop leading.

2. Let everyone know what's expected: In planning and acting strategically, you must make everyone realize what is expected of them. Everyone should know about the standards to which they are being held. If there is no law, then there is no violation. If there is no expectation, there is no performance. Put in place indices that can be

used to measure performance. Then keep an eye out for top performers. After taking out the top performers, you should give these ones extra attention and support to take them from good enough to great. Create a sort of mentorship program to further refine the skills which you have identified in them.

3. Let work be a learning curve: Work that is done for the sake of work tends to become boring after a while. You should design tasks in such a way that people are able to learn at their jobs. You should build learning periods into your work schedule. The excuse many managers and business owners give is that, there is not enough time to dabble into employee development, but I dare to say that if you lengthen the day by another 12 hours, time will still not be enough. Therefore, it all boils down to time management and how important employee development is to you. You can blur the line between learning and work. You can create an environment where the line between learning and work is blurred. If you

want to develop future leaders, you can create environments where employees work on assignments and anticipate and create solutions to challenges.

4. Encourage them to develop: Every great leader know that a successive plan is very important in the maintenance of leadership. Leaders who develop their successors have a higher likelihood of creating a high retention rate in their company. They have employees who are satisfied with their job, more productive, and more committed. This is why it is important that you keep an eye out for employees who show and live the values that are important in the achievement of the overall goal and the future of your organization. These are the people you should focus personal developmental action on. This might take time, but if you have the future in mind, you will see how it is worth it.

Development strategy

Information › Application › Duplication › Repeat

5. Protect them: It is your job as a leader to protect, support, and serve your employees as leader. It is your duty to protect them against internal/external threats like bad working environments, negative people, and burnout. As a good leader, you must set a high-performance culture that will ensure that promote good and effective relationships amongst co-workers. Your strategy must demonstrate that you have true and genuine concern for them. It must show that their effort is valued. Your environment must be one that promotes high performance, inspiration, and objectivity. Appropriate conflict resolution strategy must also be in place for any tension to be resolved. Dialogue should be a valuable tool for you to be closer to them. Let them see that you want to listen to them. When employees are sure that you are committed to them, they will commit to you.

6. Build their strength and leverage on talent:

Everyone is a 10/10 at something; your job as a leader is to find out what that thing is. Good leaders are known for recognizing, emphasizing, and leveraging talents. They are good at finding out what is working rather than focusing on weakness and what isn't working. By focusing on strengths, you are creating positivity because you can see and appreciate what is working, thereby making you get better engagement and momentum to get the result you want. This will also mean that you must address situations where there is a lapse in performance and look for ways to fix them. One of the major reasons people stay or leave an organization is their immediate boss. If you relate well with them and help them see their strength, they will stay.

7. Pass along information on opportunities for self-development

Good leaders use their positions, experience, and network to search for opportunities for their employees. Employees need to know about emerging trends, create good network, develop their career, and even change jobs. The truth is that, true leaders don't try to tie down employees even if they are the most valuable. Yes. You want to retain employees especially when you have invested heavily. But the truth is that leaving sometimes is inevitable. When this happens, you don't want to burn bridges. Instead, you want them to be your eyes and ears wherever they go to. You want to spread your influence. You want to create a network of high net-worth individual who will be easily accessible to you because you helped them get to where they are right now. Life-long loyalty should be what's on your mind instead of short term gains.

8. Let internal candidates be the first consideration for top positions

After you might have established the criteria for making the top positions and gotten all stakeholders on board, then try to get an assessment of internal candidates first before looking out. You can hire an outside firm to even carry out an independent assessment to avoid bias and favoritism if your company is a relatively large one. Consider performers in the top 20% and see if they meet the requirements for the position when creating your succession plan. It might help to test them by making them experience a simulation of what it will be like to be in the desired position. Give them stretch assignments.

Promoting candidates internally is a good motivator for employees as it will inspire them to give their best for the dream of getting to that top position in your organization. You must also evaluate before you elevate. If you are not ready, do not promote them. Instead, celebrate their small wins.

It is only after you have looked inward and can't find any successor should you start planning to bring talent from outside. When a candidate is eventually chosen for the position, then such a person should be on-boarded properly.

The truth is that, no candidate is completely ready for the tasks ahead. They will make their mistakes, learn from it, and need crucial support.

In the end, an organizational culture based on performance is very important to the achievement of mission and vision goals. But it is only through coaching, constant dialogue, good interpersonal relationship, and a working leadership plan can superior results be achieved.

Key Success Factors

1. **Planning is everything**

   The first that you must do is begin with the end in mind. Once you know the destination you can strategically chart the course.

2. **Prepare others to lead**

   "There is no success without a successor." Therefore, you must build and leverage talent to maximize the opportunity for growth. One of the worst things is for your company to be growing rapidly with no one to fill key positions.

3. **Protect your people**

   Your people are the lifeline of your organization, so you must equip your people with the necessary tools to navigate through systematic and emotional issues. Always. I repeat always evaluate before you elevate your top talent. You can lose good people by setting them up to fail in a situation they are not prepared for.

Conclusion

Like I often tell people, today matters but tomorrow matters even more. In other words, your daily decisions should lead you to your desired destination. The only way to reach that destination is to plan. Planning is managing and giving your time purpose. If you want to effectively lead others, you must master the art of planning. A leader must provide the vision, framework, and pipeline to funnel future leaders to carry the torch.

Leadership is about legacy. Everything we have discussed in this book from self-leadership to helping others see the way is about making an impact and leaving a legacy that will be talked about for generations to come.

The kind of legacy that counts, is that which relates with the development of people that are around you. Ten years from now, many of the people that surround you today will not be there any longer, but will they sing your praise wherever they are? Will they be able to fly and soar like eagles? Will they be able to take off on their own? Will they be able to attribute their success to the learning outcomes gained from their time with you? These are the questions you should ask yourself as a leader. If the people that surround you cannot do great exploit in your absence, then you have not done a good job as a leader. There are people around you that would love to benefit from your advice, wisdom, and experience. So, it's imperative that you find yourself and then lose yourself investing in others.

For me, the greatest legacy any leader can leave, is raising giants who are bigger than themselves. Use your knowledge to develop people. Let your interactions with people be a force multiplier. Invest in people as you are investing in yourself. This book has shown you many ways you can do this successfully. Also, encourage others to pass whatever knowledge they have gained to others. The people around you are the assets that matter. It is not the money or fame that you acquire. Always pay it forward.

You leave a legacy when you build people to that level where achievement and success can be obtained without you in the picture. To sum it up, leadership is about production and duplication. If you can't produce others to lead in their area of gifting, then you must look in the mirror and ask yourself, am I fit to lead in this capacity?

So, let me ask you, what do you want people to say about you when you are not there? What is your leadership legacy?

www.ingramcontent.com/pod-product-compliance
Lightning Source LLC
Chambersburg PA
CBHW070300230526
45470CB00002B/655